LOUISVILLE
Architecture and the
Urban Environment

Symbolic of the "new" Louisvi
Mies van der Rohe's American
Life Building and the First
National Bank Tower by Harris
and Abramovitz

William Morgan

LOUISVILLE

ARCHITECTURE AND THE URBAN ENVIRONMENT

Introduction by Noel Perrin

1979

William L. Bauhan, Publisher

DUBLIN, NEW HAMPSHIRE

Library of Congress Cataloging in Publication Data:

Morgan, William, 1944-
Louisville: architecture and the urban environment.
Based on author's ''Urban environment'' column in the Courier-journal, Louisville, Ky.
   Bibliography: p.
   1. Louisville, Ky.—Buildings. 2. Architecture—Kentucky—Louisville. 3. Louisville, Ky.—City planning. 4. City planning—Kentucky. I. Title.
NA735.L6M67   720'.9769'44   79-631
ISBN 0-87233-050-8

The chapters in this book originally appeared in *The Courier-Journal & Times* and *The Courier-Journal,* Louisville, Kentucky.

All photographs are by the author, except those by James Blue, page 22; Bill Strode, courtesy of the *Courier-Journal,* page 26; and Carl Maupin, page 88.

Designed by Iain Bain and W.L. Bauhan
Set in Times Roman type with titles in Melior by A & B Typesetters, Inc.
Concord, New Hampshire, and printed and bound at the Heffernan Press, Inc.
Worcester, Massachusetts, U.S.A.

For Lindsay Morgan
born in Louisville, 17 February 1977

Acknowledgments

The chapters in this book originally appeared as articles in *The Courier-Journal* in a column entitled "The Urban Environment" under the enlightened aegis of Sunday editor Geoffrey Vincent. Thanks are also due to the present Sunday editor Paul Neely, to the Sunday department's Connie Pearson, and to publisher Barry Bingham, Jr.

Many Louisvillians have been generous in sharing their ideas and greater knowledge of the city. I am especially indebted to Nancy Farnsley and Grady Clay; to Douglas Stern (now preservation officer of the City of Evansville) and Professor Joy Kloner of the University of Louisville.

It is unlikely that I should be either teaching or writing about architecture, planning, or preservation were it not for my own teachers: Hugh Morrison of Dartmouth, James Marston Fitch of Columbia, and particularly George Tatum of Delaware.

Any writing on architecture and urbanism in Louisville would be impossible without the inspiration of Charles Farnsley, former mayor, Congressman, and Louisville's greatest champion.

W.M.

Contents

List of Illustrations

Introduction

BACK IN THE FIFTIES I used to work for a magazine that was published in a New Jersey suburb called Oradell. It was really a New York magazine, but the owner had pulled it across the river into New Jersey to save taxes. This did not improve the social life of the editors. Lunch was an especial problem.

Most of the editors tried stubbornly to pretend that they were still in the city. Had they been, they would have fanned out across Manhattan for lunch each weekday: seeing old friends, making new ones, hearing the news in the world of journalism—and, incidentally, getting a good meal. As it was, about six of the ten editors went each day to a third-rate restaurant a mile from the office to sop up martinis and eat the terrible food. Two—the top two—mostly stayed in the office and worked right through.

The final two, of whom I was one, hadn't the head to drink so many martinis, nor the stomach for the food. Certainly we had no interest in donating our lunch hours to the company. The result was that three or four or sometimes even five days a week we would get a quick sandwich and then spend the rest of the hour walking the streets of Oradell. We covered all of them many times.

Early on, we began to play an architectural game. In its original form, it was very simple. We would try to agree on modern houses whose design we liked.

I recall Oradell as having had about a thousand houses of recent vintage, and I recall our having given our stamp of approval to somewhere around a dozen. This low figure came as a surprise to both of us. We became curious as to why we liked so few, and we began *really* to look at houses, and to discuss elevations, and picture windows, and small panes versus large panes. We began to be able to spot the work of different developers.

All of this was a slow and quite inarticulate process. Though we were both graduates of good colleges (Williams and Yale, to be precise), and had both taken liberals arts courses exclusively, neither of us knew a damn thing about architecture. How should we? Except for an artsy few, and a proportion of those who had been much to Europe, no American knew a damn thing about architecture. To like skyscrapers and log cabins and Gothic churches, to love Georgian architecture without being quite sure what it was, to despise split-level ranches, to fall under the spell of "Spanish-mission" on a visit to San Francisco—that was about the limit for educated Americans a quarter of a century ago.

There has been a degree of change since then. It mostly affects attitudes towards the past. A much higher proportion of Americans now know something about our architectural history. They can recognize a Federal house, or the Roman arches of a twenties football stadium. They've been to Williamsburg. They support historic preservation districts. If they're Kentuckians, they know and care about Old Louisville. This is a huge gain.

But when it comes to modern architecture, most of us remain as ignorant as the average developer. How should we not be? On the one hand, there are the architects and planners, talking a language of their own. They tell the rest of us we must admire some on-the-face-of-it dull or even ugly building. Why? Because it's "honest." Or "bold." Or because it expresses a contemporary aesthetic. Or employs space interestingly. Or because you can actually see the splayed-out grain of the plywood mold in the cast concrete wall.

On the other hand, there are the rest of us. We can accept the new aesthetic on their authority, without really understanding it (they don't explain it: they assert), or we can remain bewildered and dubious. Most of us remain bewildered and dubious.

But in very recent years new help has come our way. A few architectural critics of a new breed have appeared. They understand and love our architectural past—they are preeminent in saving it from demolition—and at the same time they understand and admire good contemporary architecture. Better yet, they can make their admiration intelligible. They can explain in ordinary language why one new courthouse is a treasure to cherish, and another is a mere trendy pastiche, or an exercise in ingenuity. They can even make sense of parking garages.

Such men and women are extremely scarce. Louisville is fortunate in having one of the best of them—the author of this book. It is equally fortunate in having a newspaper of the same high caliber, that he can write for. The paper not only permits but encourages free discussion of every aspect of construction and planning in the city, even at the risk of annoying wealthy advertisers. Morgan in the *Courier-Journal* is an event.

It is said that a people gets the government it deserves. If it is also true that a city gets the buildings and the critics and the journalism it deserves, then Louisville is a lucky place. For with intelligence like Will Morgan's directed on the future of the city, and with that intelligence serving to focus what caring people in the city feel anyway, then both the old buildings that Louisville chooses to save and the new ones it chooses to build are going to be the envy of other cities for many years to come.

Noel Perrin
Dartmouth College

Why Louisville?

LOUISVILLE is the setting of the buildings and events described in this book. But the issues it addresses are not particular to Kentucky's largest city. Exceptional as well as poor design, preservation wins and losses, and the effects of both intelligent and thoughtless planning decisions can be observed in any American city.

If Louisville shares common urban experiences with the rest of the nation's cities, it is different for the obvious reasons of geography, history, and culture. Although known throughout the world for a horse race run here every May, Louisville is also gaining a national reputation in the field of historic preservation. Old Louisville, for example, is one of the largest National Historic Districts in the country.

Louisville is also notable among cities of its size in that its highly respected newspaper has shown some concern for the visual and physical development of the region it serves. *The Courier-Journal* currently features a regular column on architecture and urban planning, and its first urban affairs editor, Grady Clay, was hired as early as 1963.

Despite *The Courier-Journal's* tradition of urban affairs reporting, architectural coverage remains a very minor segment of the usual newspaper fare. Planning and design decisions that can affect thousands, even millions, of citizens for generations to come, receive a disproportionately small amount of space compared to political events which may turn out to be far more transient in the long run. Even when measured against other reporting in the arts, architecture usually gets less notice than movies, music, opera, and even ballet; it is hard to imagine a newspaper without a television critic, yet only a handful of journals have full-time writers covering the built environment.

Architectural criticism has thus been limited to the larger newspapers which presumably can better afford to include what is too often regarded as an elitist field of little interest to most readers. All of us writing on architecture are deeply indebted to Ada Louise Huxtable, architecture critic of *The New York Times*. Another constant source of inspiration has been Wolf Von Eckardt of *The Washington Post*.

Indeed, it was a syndicated piece on the new American embassy in Moscow by Von Eckardt that prompted this writer to ask *Courier-Journal* publisher Barry Bingham, Jr., if Louisville wasn't large enough to support an architecture critic. Mr. Bingham turned the proposition over to then Sunday editor Geoffrey Vincent, who asked for a general piece (the essay that opens this book) and who gave the column its title "The Urban Environment." That first piece appeared on January 26, 1975, and, for better or for worse, the column has run ever since.

During the several years in which the pieces have appeared, new buildings, planning decisions, and other events have altered the face of the city; this time also marks changes in my own ideas on architecture and urbanism.

The buildings reviewed in that first article in 1975 were treated as individual and isolated monuments of architectural design. I still hold that the First National Tower is a handsome example of the corporate glass box, but it must also be judged in terms of its urban context. While it may be good design, it is a planning disaster. A forty-story building in a city the size of Louisville destroys the scale of downtown; it also contributes to the decline of real estate values, and thereby jeopardizes the older buildings which define the city's character.

I have also had second thoughts about so readily criticizing the penchant for erecting colonial-style buildings. As the result of academic training with men fighting the battle for modern architecture, I am still philosophically opposed to erecting buildings which ape the past, especially for building types with no historical precedents, such as gas stations, factories, or supermarkets. Still, given the continuing popularity of employing red brick and white columns, one wonders whether the colonial style has perhaps become an American vernacular, whether future historians might refer to twentieth-century architecture as the last phase of eighteenth-century Georgian.

However, the real issue is not style, but rather good design and quality of execution. There is a great difference between a scholarly and tasteful Georgian re-creation, such as Charles A. Platt's William Speed house, and a speculative suburban tract house with a quartet of badly proportioned columns applied to the facade. As the craftsmanship necessary to erect historically accurate electic buildings did not survive the Depression, a simpler, more contemporary architectural style would seem better suited to the late twentieth century.

While debate over points of style may not interest the general reader, it is hoped that any discussion of the built environment may stimulate an increased awareness of our physical resources and might lead to demands for higher standards of design. The reaction to articles, such as that regarding the future of the Big Four railroad bridge, suggests that many citizens may be more concerned and better informed about environmental design than their political leaders.

The Big Four Bridge has yet to be transformed into a unique and dramatic symbol of Louisville—our equivalent of the St. Louis Arch or the Sydney Opera House, but it is being talked about, its possible renovation is being studied, and the idea is being kept before the public.

Similarly, the city has begun to study and implement ways to use its 375 miles of alleys. And, there is the liklihood that, even if the Taylorsville Dam is not stopped, more serious considerations will be given to the consequences of sweeping land-use planning by such normally unresponsive and often publicly irresponsible agencies as the Army Corps of Engineers.

Simply stated, the purpose of the "Urban Environment" column is to remind people of the role that architecture and design have in shaping our surroundings and in determining the quality of life in this city. In doing so, it has sometimes been necessary to berate the city for its lack of imagination. But conservatism, failure of nerve, and visual illiteracy are not just Louisville limitations.

In some areas, particularly historic preservation, Louisville has a better than average record. Louisville still has a long way to go before it recovers and makes the best use of its waterfront—its *raison d'etre.* But it has had notable success in its landmarks program and in its attempts to preserve neighborhoods like Old Louisville, the Cherokee Triangle, Portland, and Butchertown.

Louisville has begun to find that in appreciating and enhancing its own architectural heritage it is also insuring its economic future, for it is becoming increasingly apparent that cities which save their old buildings and neighborhoods are also saving their downtowns. And, we would do well to remember that our monuments and our streetscapes are not that much newer or less interesting than those we so often seek as tourists in Europe. For instance, our courthouse is almost exactly contemporary with Britain's Houses of Parliament.

An architectural historian is a lucky person, for his visual training almost precludes boredom. There is rarely a city, or even a small town, that does not provide something for his heightened visual appetite. And, it was Louisville's architecture—Actors Theatre, West Main Street, Old Louisville, and the Highlands—that attracted me here. Architecture, as the physical indicator of a city's spirit, was the determining factor in my choice of Louisville over job offers in other cities.

Having chosen Louisville for its buildings, its townscape, and its ambiance, rather than for its schools, suburbs, country clubs or athletic teams—estimable as these may be—I hope to have helped preserve some of our physical heritage, past and present, for others to enjoy tomorrow. I also hope that this book may not only help make people more aware of their surroundings but may contribute to the ongoing task of environmental design. That task, as succinctly defined by Albert Eide Parr, director emeritus of the American Museum of Natural History: "is not to provide a terminal retirement home for our civilization, but to guide the evolution of our surroundings in such a manner that we may find delight and assurance both in the process and in the stages it takes us through."

William Morgan

Louisville
December 1978

I. BUILDINGS

The riverfront Belvedere
dominated by Harrison and
Abramovitz's 40-story First
National Bank Tower and before it
the American Life Building by
Mies van der Rohe

Symbols of the "New Louisville"

THE many new buildings that have arisen in downtown Louisville in the last few years are proudly pointed to as symbols of the "New Louisville"—symbols of the city's commercial rebirth and its rediscovery of the riverfront. Since the mid-1960s, over a third of a billion dollars has been spent on downtown construction, but what has been built is far more than just new real estate. Architecture by definition becomes the most visible and permanent manifestation of the idea of the "new" city, and, when added together, all of the individual buildings compose the urban environment. As Louisvillians are concerned with the city they inhabit, it is worthwhile to focus a critical eye on some of those structures that make up the Louisville environment, and in particular those that forcibly reflect the value of such a major financial commitment.

The forty-story height of the First National Bank Tower (the state's tallest building) makes it Louisville's most visible corporate symbol. The tall black slab of the First National Tower announces Louisville's presence to the motor traveler long before the rest of the city comes into view. From Sao Paulo to Montreal, tall buildings are axiomatic of a booming city. Glass boxes set in plazas have become almost a cliché, yet New York architects Harrison & Abramovitz have given Louisville one of the better examples of that genre.

First National's anodized, copper-colored metal sheathing and tinted glass read as a single flat slab. But rather than being cold and mechanical, strong contrasts are created between the sides in the sun and those in shadow. Depending on the time of day, the building's color varies from a rich warm brown to jet black. Architecturally, First National Tower is not an avant-garde design, but it is extremely well done and as the visual king-pin of the new Louisville skyline, its conservative elegance is most appropriate. Nevertheless, the energy crisis has made us question the wisdom of creating a need for extensive air-conditioning systems behind acres of glass.

The glass-wall skyscraper owes its genesis in large part to Mies van der Rohe, one of the major figures of twentieth-century design, and yet Mies's own American Life and Accident building on the Belvedere is only five stories tall. American Life, which is one of his last works, represents the essence of Mies's teaching, for this utterly simple structure is merely a box. As its "walls" are replaced entirely by window space, the building is defined primarily by its twelve supporting columns. This simplicity is deceptive however, for the architect who said: "I don't want to be intersting, I want to be good." has created an exceptionally handsome building that is of great interest. Using the Belvedere as a podium, and by raising the upper stories so that the building seems to float, Mies has produced what is virtually a classical temple. The sheltered area formed by

The steel facade and strip windows of Mies van der Rohe's American Life Building are contemporary echoes of the cast-iron commercial structures of a century ago. Photograph by James Blue

The Greater Louisville First Federal Savings and Loan Association presents an almost forbidding front, but its scale compliments neighboring older downtown buildings. Photograph by James Blue

the recessed ground floor echoes the pavillions of the Belvedere and becomes a natural extension of those human-scaled spaces. A Mies building—whether a bank, an office block, or a museum—became the urban status symbol of recent years, but Louisville's example is more than that. It is unique in its use of Cor-ten steel, a naturally rusting material that gives the building a warm patina not usually associated with steel and glass.

Similar in size and function to American Life, is the recently completed Greater Louisville First Federal Savings and Loan Association at the corner of Fourth and Market streets. But in contrast to its steel and glass neighbors, the newer building's broad, windowless stucco surfaces seems to signal a move away from the "open" financial institutions so characteristic of the late 1960s and toward the old image of solidness and security; its four massive granite-clad piers suggest reference to the earlier Greek Revival, a style synonymous with banking institutions, such as the original Bank of Louisville (now Actors Theatre).

More than an image of impregnability (for some tastes Greater Louisville may seem defensible only in a military sense), the new savings bank performs an important function in visually anchoring the corner of the block. The architects (Bank Building and Equipment Corporation of America, St. Louis) have respected the line and scale of the street, a simple but tremendously important gesture in a city whose streetscape has been increasingly eroded by parking spaces and empty lots. When viewed from across Market Street and the site of the new convention center, the bank acts as a visual base for the First National Tower. This over-all image of solidity gives way to delightful surprise when closer inspection reveals an extra floor below street level, and that one must bridge a moat to enter the building. While there are a few details that seem a bit fussy (the logo should have been left off the main wall, and not everyone likes the purple and beige color scheme), Greater Louisville is the sort of interesting and provocative solution that gives us "architecture" rather than just a building.

The major determinant that shapes so much of modern building is economics, but the clients for whom these new Louisville buildings were erected demanded structures that contribute something more than just financial return. Although it is easy to talk of the "spirit" of a city, what the visitor actually carries away with him is a visual impression. Only by continuing to stress a high level of architectural design can the new Louisville achieve a special character that will separate it from countless other new American downtowns.

Let's Save the Big Four

THE BIG FOUR BRIDGE is a symbol of this city just as Churchill Downs and the Belle of Louisville are symbols, and like them, the bridge is equally worthy of veneration. Despite the appearance of decay afflicted by neglect and disuse, and despite uninformed remarks that it is an eyesore worthy of immediate banishment to the scrapheap, the Big Four Bridge is actually an asset to be capitalized upon, a resource as full of promise as the Belle of Louisville or the Belvedere.

When speaking of architectural symbols of a city, courthouses, cathedrals, capitols—Independence Hall, the Empire State Building, the Houses of Parliament—rather than a railroad bridge come most readily to mind. We should remember however, that some of the absolute best examples of American building—and that most admired by Europeans—are utilitarian structures like grain elevators, factories, and our often very technologically-advanced bridge spans. Although not as dramatically sited as San Francisco's Golden Gate Bridge, the Big Four is a visual gateway to a city which lacks any really noteworthy topographical features, such as a magnificent harbor or a ring of mountains.

The Big Four is historically symbolic of American technological know-how, as well as of the railroad's role in Louisville's commercial growth. A locomotive long adorned the seal of the city, and just a few weeks ago the railroad's very substantial contribution to the city was formally recognized by the placing of the first Louisville Historic Landmarks plaque on Union Station. The Big Four Bridge is older than the railroad terminal, and is also older, more technologically sophisticated, and handsomer than the great symbol of Paris, the Eiffel Tower.

Even if we accept the Big Four's value as a living reminder of the city's importance as a rail center, and further agree that it is a key element of our riverscape that should be preserved, the challenge of recycling such a large and unusual structure is formidable. This is not the first time it has been suggested that the Big Four be adapted to some other use. Architects especially have long been fascinated by the unique opportunity presented by the bridge. Half-a-dozen years ago the Big Four was offered as a design problem to architecture students at the University of Kentucky by Louisville architect Jasper Ward. Some of the proposals were whimsical—a masoleum, an amusement park contained within a giant Louisville Slugger baseball bat created by wrapping the bridge in plastic—but many were practical: hotels, apartments, low-cost housing, parks, and even a recycling center where waste goods would be deposited directly into river barges. A park-like promenade would be welcome, as would a recycling center, to say nothing of the fact that Louisville's riverfront development scheme so far lacks much-needed housing. And, wouldn't a hotel right over the river be a lot more exciting and more spectacular than the atrium-style hostelry

The Big Four Railroad Bridge, visual gateway to the city

planned as part of the new convention center? Certainly, anything built on the bridge would have an unparalleled view of both the river *and* downtown—and what better spot from which to watch the great steamboat race.

To be sure, the problems of adapting the bridge to any such use are difficult, but are they insurmountable? The City of Louisville should sponsor a national (or better yet, international) architectural competition to solicit ideas for using the bridge. Such a competition would provide the city with excellent publicity, publicity that would reinforce the idea that Louisville really is an exciting, imaginative city.

The Big Four Bridge is too important an asset, historically and visually, to be squandered. There should at least be debate about the future of the bridge and exploration of possible adaptive uses. A project to preserve and develop the bridge for Louisvillians would have far more impact, far more lasting value, than the coonskin-covered, plastic Liberty Bell commemorative events produced for the Bicentennial by almost every American city and town.

POSTSCRIPT. *In 1977, the State of Kentucky awarded $50,000 (administered by the Preservation Alliance of Louisville and Jefferson County) for a feasibility study regarding structural soundness and possible re-use of the Big Four. A local development firm, Kentucky Real Estate Holding Corporation, plans a shopping and entertainment center, plus exhibition space and a hotel on the bridge; six major hotel chains have expressed interest in the bridge. It also appears that the city may obtain ownership of the bridge as payment for back taxes owned by Penn Central.*

The Louisville skyline at dusk serves as a background to the Big Four Bridge. Citizens Plaza building is at left, First National Tower in the center. Beyond the Big Four is the Kennedy Bridge. Photograph by Bill Strode, courtesy of *The Courier-Journal*

Cast-Iron Architecture

ARCHITECTURE plays a major role in the image of, and in the perception of, a city. And given Louisville's nationally recognized efforts to preserve its architectural heritage, perhaps one should ask: What is its chief claim to architectural fame? Rather than the Victorian houses in Old Louisville, Farmington or Locust Grove, the new downtown skyscrapers or Churchill Downs, the answer is unquestionably the city's nineteenth-century cast-iron commercial buildings.

There are probably two dozen or more cast-iron structures (or buildings with partial or complete cast-iron fronts) downtown. Most of them, like the Carter Dry Goods Building and the Hart Block, are in the recently expanded Main Street Historic District. There are a few scattered examples along Market and Fourth streets (opposite the new Convention Center). Main Street, especially, is nationally known and is a featured Louisville attraction in such guides as those published by gasoline companies. The Metropolitan Preservation Plan published here in 1973 stated that "Main Street is the most impressive and continuous visual record of a nineteenth-century city's commercial activity in existence." Cast-iron buildings are the primary reason for such an accolade, and many warehouses are being renovated now along Main Street.

Basically, cast-iron architecture has achieved a prominent place in the development of American architecture because it is generally accepted as the forerunner of the steel-framed skyscraper and as an early example of prefabrication and standardized modular design.

But the real reasons for the use of cast iron and its successes as a building material were less prescient. When employed for commercial and warehouse buildings, cast iron offered a number of advantages, not the least of which was that it was much less expensive than masonry construction. Unlike stone, which had to be quarried, cut and laboriously laid up, cast iron was mass produced—literally cast in a mold. Cast iron was lighter and stronger than masonry, and because of its strength, it did not take up as much wall space, allowing larger windows and therefore better-lighted interiors. Ornament, which had to be individually carved on a stone building, was also mass produced, and its profusion and elaboration were limited only by imagination.

Cast iron was cheaper and easier to erect, and as it was produced in endlessly repeatable sections, an architect was not required. Cast-iron buildings could be ordered directly from a catalogue and could be shipped and erected anywhere in the United States or the world—and were. The iron work that is so characteristic of New Orleans, for example, came mostly from foundries in northern cities such as Philadelphia or New York.

Cast-iron facade from James Bogardus's influential book *Cast-Iron Buildings: Their Construction and Advantages*, 1856

There were a number of catalogues offering cast-iron building designs, perhaps the most famous being *Illustrations of Iron Architecture Made by the Architectural Iron Works of the City of New York,* published in 1865 by that firm's president, Daniel D. Badger. With such catalogues a builder in any city could select the desired facade (almost invariably with Renaissance Revival style arches and columns) for any size building he needed, usually in typical twenty-five-foot-wide units with three or four bays. A bolder builder might also order iron framing members, but generally the cast-iron facade was applied to the front of a masonry building.

A competitor of Badger, James Bogardus, also of New York, claimed to be the inventor and even secured a patent. In a pamphlet he issued in 1856, called *Cast Iron Buildings: Their Construction and Advantages,* Bogardus announced that "such buildings combine unequaled advantages of ornament, strength, durability, and economy; whilst they are, at the same time, absolutely secure against danger from fire, lightning, and an imperfect foundation."

Cast-iron construction may have been economical, but fireproof it was not. It had other disadvantages. Because it was cast (as opposed to wrought), the iron had little tensile (or pulling) strength, so it could not be used for big spans, whether for framing or for facades. The fairly small individual units were thus repeated over and over, with an effect not unlike that of the contemporary curtain wall. Today's tall buildings, like the Citizens Fidelity Tower, tend to endlessly repeat one unadorned module, resulting in unmitigated boredom. Whereas, the repetition of elaborately detailed cast iron units, like those employed on the Hart Block contributes to an effect of unparalleled richness.

While Badger hoped to sell entire buildings (or at least fronts), local builders only had to borrow from his or his rivals' catalogues, for an industrial town like Louisville had its own foundries to cast the necessary building parts. Louisville's cast-iron buildings feature the elaborate detailing and the column-and-arch motif so characteristic of cast iron architecture everywhere, but most local examples were fabricated here. The foundries, as well as architects, were often identified by plaques that can still be seen on a few buildings on West Main Street.

The great age of cast iron, beginning in New York in the 1850s, coincided in Louisville with expansion of the city southward away from the river. As retail merchants moved to Market Street, wholesale businesses moved into Main Street, and cast iron was most often used for warehouses. Even though Bogardus had suggested cast iron for buildings such as houses and churches, like other technologically innovative construction of the nineteenth century, cast iron was never very popular with the public at large and tended to be relegated to more utilitarian structures.

Main Street in the second half of the nineteenth century experienced many changes, as a result of economics and natural disasters like fires. Many of the city's leading architects (among them, John Andrewartha, Henry Whitestone and D. X. Murphy) contributed buildings to the street, but as cast iron's fireproof claims were proved otherwise, many

Cast-iron facade of Charles D.
Meyer's Hart Block as seen from
the Natural History Museum

Detail of Charles D. Meyer's Hart
Block

replacements were masonry. However, C. J. Clarke employed cast iron as decoration and for the first floor facade of the Carter Dry Goods Building (Louisville's new Natural History Museum), and the most impressive building on the street, Charles D. Meyer's Hart Block, has a complete cast-iron facade.

Generally, anonymous commercial builders and enterpreneurs were responsible for the cast-iron districts that lined this and the waterfront areas of other Midwestern cities. And as the city moved away from the Ohio River towards Broadway, new construction along Main Street ceased. Ironically, Louisville's position as a languishing Southern city in the early and mid-twentieth century meant that a sizable concentration of these monuments was spared. St. Louis and Cincinnati destroyed their cast-iron legacies, and now Louisville is surpassed in its number of cast-iron buildings only by New York.

To protect New York's cast-iron heritage and to foster a greater appreciation of the buildings' role in that city's history, an organization called Friends of Cast Iron Architecture was formed. Its members receive magnetized membership cards to enable them to ascertain whether a building is cast iron.

Concern for Louisville's architectural heritage is most vociferously expressed by the Preservation Alliance, a consortium of neighborhood groups, historical societies and civic organizations interested in preserving and utilizing the city's historical buildings. As part of Alliance efforts to raise public awareness of the city's rich patrimony, it has sponsored a series of Heritage Hikes. One such hike through downtown featured the cast-iron buildings on Main Street and attracted 1,500 participants.

Through the combined efforts of the Preservation Alliance, some architects, a few businesses, and others, what remains of Main Street is being preserved and revitalized. Sadly, the cast iron and commercial buildings that still stand on Main Street represent only a shadow of what once was a truly remarkable monument to American architectural genius.

Cast-iron buildings in the 600 block of West Main Street

Faint Praise for the New Museum

LOUISVILLE'S Museum of Natural History and Science opened in the summer of 1977 with a great deal of fanfare, self-congratulation, and excitement. Most exciting is the fact that the museum's new home on West Main street is itself a museum piece. The establishment of the new cultural facility in the Carter Dry Goods building marks the climax of efforts to revitalize Louisville's cast iron district.

It is not the "first museum in the country to move into a rehabilitated historic building" (as sometimes claimed), but it is nonetheless a three-dimensional history lesson, as well as another visible symbol of the city's faith in downtown. However, now that the future of West Main street is fairly secure, one might have wished that the old museum at Fifth and York streets had been renovated, thereby injecting new life into a neighborhood far more needing of such a public commitment.

Might-have-beens aside, the restored Carter Dry Goods building has become Louisville's newest public structure. Behind the familiar cast iron and limestone facade is a major civic monument that should be analyzed, not only as an example of restoration, but as a work of contemporary architecture.

Wisely, the architects (the local firm of Louis & Henry) left the old front pretty much intact. However, the use of dark, mullionless glass, especially in the three adjoining buildings, demonstrates a lack of understanding of the nature of nineteenth-century commercial architecture, and along with the empty windows of the museum, interrupts the rhythm of the streetscape. Although adaptive re-use is a good idea—and a popular one, it does not necessarily follow that all restoration is by definition good.

The architects at least separated the new building from the old—both physically and stylistically. And they should be commended for not attempting to create a cutesy turn-of-the-century gaslight ambience. But their new facade behind the old one, with its mirror and aluminum surfaces, represents a slick exercise in a trendy 1920s revival style that is more appropriate to a fashionable discotheque than to the older structure which it joins and should visually support.

It has become fashionable for avant-garde American architects to revive the details characteristic of the International Style of the 1920s and 30s—particularly the work of men like Le Corbusier and Mies van der Rohe. Machine-aesthetic materials like chromium and glass, as well as port-hole doors and thin railings (reminiscent of the popular nautical motifs employed in the 1920s), have been used almost willy-nilly, divorced from the philosophical rationale behind their original deployment. It is almost as if architects approach design as dressmakers rather than builders.

[34]

Museum of Natural History, the
former Carter Dry Goods Building

In the hands of the leading practitioners of the style (known as "The New York School"), like Richard Meier (designer of the Atheneum for New Harmony, Indiana), this trendy style is not without some intellectual appeal. A good example of the style is the Fodrea Elementary School in nearby Columbus, designed by Caudill, Rowlett, Scott, and the winner of two national design awards.

Generally, contemporary architecture in Louisville is about ten or twenty years behind New York and Europe, and so perhaps we ought to welcome the introduction of current fashion here. Yet, in the hands of Louis & Henry, this use of 1970s modernism becomes a meaningless exercise in keeping up with the architectural Joneses.

The museum has become one of the cultural metaphors of the mid-twentieth century, and we can be grateful that Louisville has been spared one of the pompous marble boxes with white columns that curse so many American cities. Still, one of the cardinal rules of museum design ought to be that the building should serve as the backdrop for the exhibits.

Instead of a simply strong statement that would do just that, we are given futuristic aluminum-corduroy-covered walls and space-age materials more suited to *Star Wars* than to our river valley heritage. In what can be seen only as an ironic misunderstanding of the nautical motifs of the 1920s, every non-aluminum surface is painted or carpeted in a deadening battleship-gray color.

The centerpiece of the museum interior is billed as a "spectacular" atrium. While it is potentially an exciting open space, it is frighteningly similar to the hotel lobbies of the Hyatt chain. It needs only the addition of a glass-encased elevator to make it a scalded-down copy of the new Hyatt hotel at Fourth and Jefferson streets.

Still, the fact that a notable nineteenth-century commercial structure has been preserved and given new life as a place to display the artifacts of our past and to interpret our history is no mean achievement. But it is sad that the local architectural profession did not rise to the task of respecting and building upon the museum's chief attraction.

The interior of the Museum is separated physically and stylistically from the old, exterior portion

Non-Architecture:
the Mini-Courthouse

JEFFERSON COUNTY is one of the most important architectural patrons in the Louisville area. Because of its very public nature, any new government-sponsored construction is of great interest. While taxpayers (who paid for, and will presumably benefit from new buildings) are concerned with how their dollars are spent, they also have the right as citizens to expect a symbolic value that supersedes monetary considerations. Therefore, local government has a great responsibility to commission and build the highest quality architecture possible. In its latest projects, Jefferson County has both lived up to—and, in some cases, failed miserably—in facing that responsibility. ——

The new Jefferson Hall of Justice, opposite City Hall, promises to be a worthy successor to the handsome courthouse which has admirably symbolized county government since its design in 1835 by the noted Greek Revival architect Gideon Shryock. The work of Design Associates (a consortium of five local architectural firms), the Hall of Justice is a Brutalist-style building that should be one of Louisville's architectural landmarks. Its strong, massive forms will nicely complete a significant government complex including City Hall, the old courthouse, and the old jail (which should definitely be preserved).

Unlike so many public structures built in recent years, the Hall of Justice was designed from the inside out, rather than as a pre-conceived monument into which various functions are then squeezed as an afterthought. In this case, these functions—police headquarters, corrections departments and jail, and various courts—are clearly articulated on the exterior, with the more public spaces being emphasized. In this respect, the Hall of Justice, like the Louisville Free Public Library and the Humanities Building at the University of Louisville, is indebted to the Boston City Hall, designed by Kallman, McKinnell and Knowles in 1963. Boston's very influential building was the result of a competition. And although the Jefferson Hall of Justice perhaps more closely resembles some of the rejected designs for that building, it is an example of first-rate architecture worthy of a great city.

Comparison of the excellent Hall of Justice with the recently completed Jefferson County Southwest Government Center reveals the latter to be a painfully weak building. In contrast with the downtown work of Design Associates the county's new "mini-courthouse" by Kenneth Mock and Raymond Berry cannot even be called "architecture." It is rather construction, and not much better than most of the speculative strip building that already crowds Dixie Highway. For almost a million dollars we are given a 100-foot-square brick building that might be mistaken for an apartment block of the sort spawned by the Watterson Expressway.

The Jefferson County Southwest Government Center on the Dixie Highway, completed in 1975

[38]

Presumably, what is supposed to tell us that the new government center is a public building is the portico with its four Ionic columns, in the so-called "colonial" style. Does this sort of trite symbolism really express county government in the 1970s? Doesn't "colonial" refer to that period when we were under the domination of a foreign monarch? Perhaps the imagery that this building is supposed to evoke is a mixture of the two periods, like having Patrick Henry or Thomas Jefferson take time from the struggle for independence to pick up their new license plates. While good architecture can enhance and enrich the life of the user, the new courthouse, with its motel-like interior and nine-foot ceilings, offers only boredom. The focal point of the major courtroom (itself a depressing, windowless box) is a thirty-foot mural of George Rogers Clark by John Alwes, a piece of art that compares with this year's Greater Louisville phone book cover as the worst historical painting of recent memory. In short, the Southwest Government Center is not only an architectural failure, it is an embarrassment and an insult to the community it was designed to serve.

If such criticism seems harsh, one needs only to look at the county's new Detoxification Center on Preston Street. Only slightly larger than the mini-courthouse, the Detoxification Center offers 81 beds and extensive rehabilitation facilities in a handsome building, complete with exciting interior spaces and a vibrant and cheerful color scheme. Designed by Carleton Godsey, this reinforced-concrete and brick structure proves that the county can provide architecture that is both attractive and functional.

It remains puzzling that the citizens of the Shively area are given Disneyland Colonial when the county has demonstrated that it can be a discriminating patron. The mini-courthouse is the first of three identical ones, but it is unfortunate that for the other two government centers the county will not follow the high standard set by the downtown buildings and abandon the lowest-common-denominator style of the Mock and Berry design.

What Do You Mean Colonial?

ONE OF THE most curious and unsettling aspects of the recent Bicentennial was that the celebration served to obscure and cheapen our heritage, rather than elucidating it and making it more meaningful. The plague of plastic eagles and red-white-and-blue everything, from license plates to underwear, attests to the commercialization of our history.

Unfortunately this debasement of our past is apparent in the all-too-visible and permanent objects of our society, its architecture. Perhaps then, we should pause and briefly examine what constitutes our "colonial" architectural heritage, and how we are venerating it or defaming it.

Even the work "colonial" has been so overused and abused that it has been rendered meaningless: we know only that it refers to brick buildings with porticos and that it is somehow patriotic. As an architectural definition, historians use "colonial" to refer to the buildings of the American Colonies constructed in the seventeenth century. "Georgian" is the term used to describe the architecture of the eighteenth century, presumably the period that present day "colonial" is attempting to evoke.

The architectural styles of both centuries were brought from Europe, and thus cannot be called particularly American. The settlers of New England erected wood-framed, medieval-proportioned houses similar to those they had known in the timber-building regions of England whence they emigrated. Only as winters proved too rigorous did they cover their half-timbering with clapboards and make other such environmental adaptions.

Settlers in Virginia built with brick, which was familiar to them in the brick-building areas of the mother country. Settlers in Pennsylvania continued a masonry building tradition. The log cabin—that most "American" of buildings—was also an importation, introduced by the Swedes and the Finns.

Relatively few buildings remain from the seventeenth century, so it is eighteenth-century architecture that we generally think of as Early American. The style properly known as Georgian represented the more sophisticated, less vernacular style of English architecture which was influenced by the Italian Renaissance. American regional differences tended to disappear in the 18th century and the main emphasis was on proportion, symmetry and classical details, such as columns and pediments.

Unquestionably, eighteenth-century America produced some outstanding architecture of which we can be justifiably proud. But it must be reiterated that the Georgian style was English in inspiration and in substance.

For truly American architecture, we must look to the nineteenth

The Bardstown Road branch of
the First National Bank of
Louisville, built in 1975, is an
underscaled version of the
Governor's Palace at
Williamsburg

Opposite.
Gasoline station in the "Colonial"
mode

century. That was when American builders, using European precedents as a starting point and not as a straitjacket, began freely creating uniquely American styles. The result was wonderfully expressive exercises such as the Louisville City Hall (with its marvelous iconographic program of horses, cows, mules and pigs) and the old Louisville Water Works on River Road.

America's creative genius and its growing industrial might were demonstrated even more forcefully by less consciously architectural work: factories, grain elevators and commercial blocks (such as those lining Main Street). Technological developments, like the steel frame, plate glass (first produced across the river in New Albany) and the elevator, all added to America's major contribution to world architecture: the skyscraper.

Yet today we decorate houses, supermarkets, filling stations and all kinds of structures with incongruous plastic balustrades and cupolas (for hanging Paul Revere's lanterns?), instead of continuing the nineteenth-century spirit of creativity and pioneering technological development.

Certainly we should praise and protect the architecture of our Founding Fathers, but we perpetuate the worst with an architecture that weakly borrows details, while failing to capture anything of the spirit that infused the original sources.

Outside of architecture, the term "colonial" usually carries a derogatory connotation. Curious then, that when Washington welcomes foreign leaders including those of new nations just freed from the bonds of a less-endearing colonialism, the policy is to take them not to New York (cultural capital of the world) or to Louisville (to see the cast-iron buildings or our great collection of Victorian architecture), but to Colonial Williamsburg, to be driven in horse-drawn carriages and attended to by "darkies" in powdered wigs.

Not only have we failed to honor the architectural spirit of our forefathers, we have made it harder for current and future generations to understand the past. The construction of a bank or any new building as a watered-down version of Independence Hall or as a pale echo of Monticello is a trade-in on our heritage which also tends to cheapen the originals.

New Music School for the Blind

IN OCTOBER 1977, just two days after the announcement of plans for the construction of a multi-million-dollar cultural center in downtown Louisville, the Music Building and Auditorium of the Kentucky School for the Blind on Frankfort Avenue was dedicated.

Since the new music building features a 300-seat auditorium and performance hall, it is of interest not only in reference to the performing-arts complex planned for Sixth and Main, but also to the University of Louisville's music school soon to be erected on the Belknap Campus. But aside from its relationship to similar planned music facilities, the Blind School's new building is worthy of recognition in its own right, for it is undoubtedly the most notable example of contemporary architecture built in Louisville in recent years.

Like so much of the work produced by the office of Jasper Ward, the new music school presents an unassuming exterior. And, unlike so much contemporary construction, it does not shout for attention. Rather, it is a compatible neighbor which sensitively blends well with the other brick structures on the Kentucky School for the Blind campus.

Constructed of a terra-cotta colored brick, the new music school faces Frankfort Avenue with a facade not unlike a classical temple. Its simple but strong colonnade makes a respectful reference to the original School for the Blind, a monumental Greek Revival building erected in 1855 and, sadly, torn down several years ago.

This colonnade—which pierces the wall instead of projecting from it—plus the glass-covered hallway on the rear, are just about the only elements which interrupt the simple, box-like masses of the building.

This simplicity is far from boring, for the sharp edges created by the unarticulated corners give the feeling that the brick is not solid or weighty, but rather a thin skin stretched tautly across the building's surface. The deep recesses of the colonnade give a sense of mystery, while an observer's movement around the building causes the openings to change in relationship to one another, resulting in a dynamism and a rhythm not unlike a musical scale.

The consciously plain exterior, as well as the greenhouse-like glass skylights on the back, give the building a certain industrial flavor. The similarities to factory architecture are emphasized even more on the interior, where the exposed plumbing is painted bright colors. This color scheme is more than just an example of the trendy "exposed-pipe school" of Pop architecture, for the colors all have a purpose as part of an architectural program based upon the needs of the clients, a majority of whom have only partial vision.

These colors act as a guide to different functions:

Yellow is to identify the choral areas (which include a forty-two-seat

Music Building and Auditorium at
the Kentucky School for the Blind
designed by Jasper Ward. A
notable example of contemporary
architecture

hall-classroom), while bright red is for exits, a lighter red is for band and instrumental areas, and orange is for public spaces. Blue and green are reserved for heating and cooling, pipes and ducts.

But the colors serve a far more important psychological role in establishing an air of brightness and exuberance.

Orange, for example, is used in the main auditorium, where painted truss-work offsets the cinder-block walls; the intensity of the orange accoustical panels on the walls and ceiling subtly changes, depending on their distance from the stage. The auditorium, built in traditional concert-hall "double cube" configuration (40 x 40 x 80 feet), is an accoustical marvel.

Whimsical gooseneck lamps (also painted orange and looking as though they were borrowed from a trolley station) line the vestibule outside the auditorium. The building's main entrance and lobby, this two-story space is also flanked by brick arcades that echo those of the exterior. In the center of this atrium is a red elevator in a yellow shaft.

Through the arcade opposite the auditorium entrance doors one can glimpse the multi-colored practice rooms, as well as the yellow choral and red band rooms. The two-story hallway running between these warm and friendly practice cubicles and the atrium is covered by a glass roof which makes the whole interior even lighter and brighter.

The Kentucky School for the Blind's new music building confirms what many astute local architecture watchers have known for a long time: Jasper Ward and his project architect, Robert Kingsley, are far and away the most imaginative and exciting architects in this city.

Occasional works like the music school demonstrate that Louisville is capable of producing buildings of national quality; this understated masterpiece is certainly the equal of many of the buildings that have made Columbus, Indiana, an architectural showcase.

Most of all, the music school of the Kentucky School for the Blind reminds us that architecture can be a joyful experience. The measure of the genius of this building is that, in successfully providing a pleasant environment for those with impaired vision, it also visually enriches the sighted.

POSTSCRIPT. *The new music building at the Blind School was the recipient of a Kentucky Society of Architects Honor Award for 1977 and was featured in the April 1978 issue of* Progressive Architecture *devoted to design for the handicapped.*

II. PLACES

A Concrete Mausoleum in the Heart of Louisville

FOLLOWING the "downtown Louisville follies" is no longer amusing. It is also getting expensive. What had been somewhat entertaining burlesque has become the blues: The city of Louisville has decided to cough up three and a half million dollars to build a garage—a concrete mausoleum for 650 cars, not just downtown, but in the very center of its civic heart.

While downtown Louisville may need more garage space, choosing the location at Sixth and Jefferson is like building a fast-food hamburger franchise across the street from Independence Hall or the White House.

The site is the visual and geographical focal point of what has been called one of the finest groupings of civic architecture in the United States. To offset Gideon Shryock's Court House, John Andrewartha's City Hall, D. X. Murphy's County Jail, the surprisingly handsome new Hall of Justice and the statues of Thomas Jefferson and Louis XVI with a garage is a slap in the face of Louisville.

The city's decision to build the garage is another example of the blind and insensitive planning that obscures our true urban potential and keeps us a regional backwater when we could and ought to be a great city.

It is hard to think of an exciting major city's being so callous and irresponsible about one of its greatest civic and visual assets. Imagine what Vienna or Paris—or even Cincinnati—would do with such a location. What Louisville is planning is both incredible and unthinkable, yet the asinine and the thoughtless are sadly what we have come to expect of planning in Louisville.

The argument that is constantly put forth about saving the city center is that we have to bring people downtown. For some reason, the corollary to this argument is that we need more parking, that is, not really people, but cars.

Downtown, in fact, needs more people, but more people who live there and a more efficient (and, if need be, free) transit system to put them there. The only thing that can be positively said of another garage in downtown is that it will contribute more congestion and increase pollution.

Traffic engineering is really not that different from the age-old science of hydraulics. However, our traffic engineers don't seem to understand the basic concept that traffic, like water, seeks its own level. More highways and more garages do not alleviate traffic; they increase it—a lesson that the Watterson Expressway well illustrates.

And some of the basic tenets of urban planning are also age-old: The scale for a city ought to be based on the pedestrian; instead, it is being based on the automobile. The same machine that allowed the development of the suburbs (places where people gladly give up a sizable portion of the countryside they sought for asphalt to park the vehicles

that take them away from the city) is now shaping downtown. What else but a suburban (or should we say "anti-urban"?) mentality would use the best piece of land for the parking of cars?

Mayor Harvey Sloane has said that the property at Sixth and Jefferson, which costs thirty-five dollars a square foot, is too expensive to be only a park or a plaza. The truth is that the space is too valuable to the city as part of its civic center, as part of its identity, to be pawned for the convenience of commuters.

Now that the city is almost two hundred years old, it is time for us to realize that the city is mature enough to demand innovative planning, planning based on human needs, not on the automobile.

POSTSCRIPT. *Shortly after this article appeared in August 1976, the City of Louisville dropped plans for the garage. Jefferson County announced that the space would be developed as a park, the centerpiece of the Jefferson Square project involving restoration of the Courthouse and the renovation of the Old Jail.*

Site of the proposed 650-car parking garage at Sixth and Jefferson across from the new Hall of Justice, left, and City Hall, right. Although now planted as a mini-park, this civic plaza demands monumental sculpture or a grand fountain

City Planning is a Job for All Sides

STATEMENTS on the Forum page of *The Courier-Journal*—that by architect Hunter Louis concerning the need for planning in downtown Louisville and the rebuttal by Citizens Fidelity Corporation Chairman Maurice Johnson—are the kind of debate that is too often lacking in this city. Such an exchange of ideas should be a regular occurrence rather than an occasional event.

While neither article was a definitive statement on planning in Louisville, together they point up the lack of an overall planning philosophy. More immediately, they stress the need for some sort of regular forum where such issues can be discussed, a vehicle to harness Louisville's considerable but too often demoralized design talent.

Mr. Louis spoke in terms of architecture, but it is men like Mr. Johnson who, though not trained in architecture, planning or aesthetics, really plan Louisville. Money is power, and by providing it—or withholding it—banks are the single most important force in city planning.

No one expects bankers to have had such training, and certainly no one questions Mr. Johnson's motives, but his piece raises more questions than it answers.

It is true that cities like Newark and Detroit "have long since lost their opportunity to save and revive their downtowns," but how did this happen?

How much did the money brokers contribute to these urban disasters by putting their mortgage money in new suburban development? How willing were they to lend money to rehabilitate older homes in the inner city? And how much of Louisville's current problems are the result of money going to the suburbs instead of to downtown?

And why have Denver and Minneapolis made it, while Detroit and Newark have not?

In many ways Louisville is closer to the two dying cities. Among other things, it has a relatively large black population. Mr. Johnson touches on an age-old planning axiom when he assesses a city's vitality by the number of women who shop in downtown. And one reason that women don't come downtown, why they prefer Oxmoor and Bashford Manor, is that the River City Mall is frequented by the black people that whites fled to the suburbs to avoid.

Are we, in effect, saying that we want not just "people" downtown, but nice, white people?

So, instead of recognizing and experiencing the vibrancy and successful urban quality of the Mall, with its many handsome buildings (just look above street level), we grope for a grand solution, an imported, grafted-on panacea like the proposed "galleria." Such a project might indeed be the right "keystone" for downtown development, but are we at the same time failing to see the many smaller pieces that make up the total mosaic of a city?

Chilling talk of "creating a completely new environment" downtown suggests that we ought to obliterate our identity, the physical "memories" that tell us who we are. No one condones the saving of "unproductive" structures, but who decides what criteria make a building unproductive, and who makes the decisions on what will go and what will replace it?

Accepting the need for the new, we still deserve the best in planning, the best new buildings and spaces possible. Instead of aspiring to the best, Louisville gets the lowest-common-denominator designs—buildings that are watered-down versions of economically productive but boring boxes in other cities. And when a "people place" like the Belvedere is built, it is compromised by two levels of roadways that come between the people and the river.

We are selling our city short when we think that bankers, lawyers, and politicians can plan the city. They can't. But architects, planners, and other visually literate people cannot do it by themselves either. If Louisville's planning is to become more than a spiritually deadening exercise in economics, cash flow, and supply and demand, both groups must work together.

Downtown:
Money or Good Taste?

IT APPEARS that grand, large-scale plans are finally going to be effected to boost the fortunes of downtown Louisville.

A Canadian developer, Oxford Properties, Ltd., has been selected for the multi-million-dollar galleria project and plans are also being proffered for the development of the Shippingport Square area along Main Street at the riverfront.

While the news that such projects are approaching the drawing-board stage is to be welcomed, there is still reason for skepticism and a need for caution, particularly in the way development is being planned. This is especially true concerning what seems to be the basic philosophy behind this planning: New is better, with prime consideration being given to money.

Obviously, when such huge sums, literally hundreds of millions of dollars, are at stake, it is understandable that bankers and business leaders are in the forefront of planning. But, as this observer has inquired so often in the past, why should this small, visually-untrained group bear sole responsibility for decisions that will affect the look of this city for generations to come?

No one questions the good intentions of the money men, and in fact the committee that selected the developers for the galleria has expressed its intention to gather some public opinion regarding the development plans.

But there remains the nagging feeling that the general philosophy behind such planning is unenlightened, old-fashioned and borrowed from other cities. It may be far less than the exciting, bold, and imaginative solutions that Louisville deserves and that would really have the best chance of insuring its special urban character.

This feeling was reinforced—to this writer at least—by a meeting where two members of the development firm and two of their associated architects met with a handful of civic leaders and preservationists to discuss the Galleria project.

When questioned about the fact that most of Oxford's successful (or at least, better-known) downtown development schemes were for northern cities—Edmonton, Calgary, Minneapolis—and how this related directly to Louisville, the designer from the presigious firm of Skidmore, Owings, and Merrill replied that indeed Louisville did have the same extremes of climate!

Both the architects (after studying Louisville for two days) and the developers stated their strong conviction that, whatever form their proposal took, it must be something big and something done all at once.

While most would agree that a huge building project, built and opened with a lot of fanfare, would be a dramatic gesture to signal the rebirth of downtown, these outside experts seemed to feel that this was the *only* way to revitalize Louisville's city center.

Even allowing for the experience gained from major projects in other cities, one cannot help but ask whether such bricks-and-mortar solutions decided in board rooms will really take into consideration that Louisville is probably the best surviving 19th-century commercial city in America. As such, its special character and its older buildings—not just dollars and cents return for the moneymen—must be the keystone of downtown planning.

It was also apparent that plans for the development project would be based heavily upon new parking facilities. Surely, we could hope for a more flexible, more open-minded approach that might consider alternative ways to preserve downtown without covering it with asphalt?

If we define a city that provides a truly urban experience as one where planning is based on the pedestrian and on density so great as to invite constant human contact, then planners should be mapping out an area of downtown that is free from the automobile.

In short, we need a dense, compact shopping district that would provide the necessary intensity, excitement, and human mix—planning that would put Louisville in the vanguard of imaginative people-based design, rather than just copying solutions of other cities.

Instead, there lurks an anti-urban philosophy that dreams of garage parking for the convenience of suburbanites, built at the expense of our ambiance and our cultural heritage.

It is admittedly easy for one interested critic to fault individual aspects of developers' and architects' ideas, but anyone who is concerned about the fate of downtown Louisville should question any such proposals. Louisville should be grateful that major developers feel that the city warrants their support and investment, but willingness to invest private dollars does not automatically insure a free hand to shape the face of the city.

POSTSCRIPT. *Proponents continue to offer rosy visions of the Galleria's future, but problems with land acquisition, funding, and the inability to secure a major department store, as well as opposition by preservationists, have slowed the project, allowing hope that Louisville's leaders might think of some sensible, less destructive way to save the city.*

A Galleria: at What Cost?

THE PLANS UNVEILED for the first phase of the proposed Galleria for downtown Louisville appeared to offer something for everyone.

Boosters of new construction were pleased by the prospect of a new office tower, department store and garages, along with plans for additional structures later. Preservationists were happy to learn that important older buildings were to be an integral part of the new plans.

Yet at the risk of dampening some of the euphoria and perhaps even endangering the welcome spirit of accommodation, we at least ought to take a serious look at those buildings that are to be demolished to make way for the Galleria.

It should be remembered that the developer's original scheme called for leveling every building in the Walnut-Liberty-Third-Fifth-Street area except the Starks Building and the Cathedral of the Assumption. That, after a public outcry, the developers should decide not to raze the old Courier-Journal (Will Sales) building, one of the city's most historic structures, and the Kaufman-Straus store, "one of the handsomest, best-executed and most representative examples of Chicago School Architecture in America," should hardly be regarded as a great victory for preservation. Such obvious landmarks should never have even been considered bargaining chips.

Even the most diehard preservationist would never profess that all old buildings ought to be kept or that structures that have outlived their usefulness should not be replaced. The real issue, however, is how much of Louisville's special commercial character we can afford to sacrifice for strictly economic gain.

There are some very handsome buildings along the River City Mall, and a look above the later additions that mar the storefronts along the west side of the 400 block of the Mall reveals some incredible visual treasures. For example, 424 (Gallenkamp's) and 440 (Dollar General Store), are examples of Art Deco, the 1930s modern style. At 456 (Super High Fashion) there is what must be a unique stained-glass window in the shape of a globe.

The corner building at the Mall and Walnut that housed the Gus Mayer store has an elaborate tile cornice and a very attractive columned window treatment. More important, it is a natural compliment in scale and decoration to the Starks Building, Stewart's and the Seelbach Hotel—all of which will remain.

Farther along Walnut toward Fifth Street is the Molee Building, with its bright-colored Hispanic tiles and pronounced copper cornice. The eleven-story Republic Building, next door at Fifth and Walnut echoes the scale of Kentucky Towers, and its rich and abundant decorative details

Detail of the endangered Gus Mayer Building at Fourth and Walnut Streets

Opposite.
Storefronts in the 400 block of River City Mall in danger of demolition to make way for the new Galleria

cause one to ask whether a new tall block here would offer such visual delight.

On Fifth Street, flanking the Cathedral of the Assumption, the Victorian Gothic rectory and the Italianate house behind The Record Publishing office are quite handsome reminders of Louisville's nineteenth-century heritage.

Almost all of the buildings along the Mall and Walnut Street slated for demolition provide a treat for the senses, as well as a link with the past. Together they make up a notable collection of early twentieth century commercial architecture characterized by an attention to detail and craftsmanship rarely equalled since.

In planning a city, oftentimes we have to trade off older buildings for new ones. But even without making an appeal for the outright preservation of these structures, we owe it to ourselves and to future generations of Louisvillians to be absolutely certain that any new buildings we erect will be better than those which we give up.

POSTSCRIPT. *The Galleria developers still would like to raze the old Courier-Journal building in order to build a skyscraper of incredibly boring design. Other structures remain threatened, but use of the once-empty Gus Mayer building and the purchase of the Seelbach Hotel by a sympathetic developer support the re-use of existing buildings as one of the chief ways to revitalize downtown.*

[59]

Building facades along the 600
block of River City Mall

Living Downtown Enlivens It

IF DOWNTOWN LOUISVILLE is to survive, it needs people who live downtown. It is a basic planning principle that a vital, stable, and safe downtown needs residents as well as workers, and places for people to live as well as hotels, convention centers, and cultural facilities. For, above all, the city is people.

How then can we attract new residents to center city? What will make the suburbanite abandon his cosy colonial or his condominium in favor of a downtown apartment? What could persuade the exurbanite to trade the shopping malls, freeway driving, and power mowers for the human interaction, the convenience, and the excitement of center city living?

For a starter, how about a block in the heart of downtown where there are no cars, five small parks, trees, an outdoor café, and a fountain? Add to these urban amenities movie theatres, restaurants, and stores, and a location less than a block away from symphony, opera, and a major public library. Then add police protection, the ethnic and social mix of a bustling city, and—not least of all—some of the most delightful commercial architecture around.

This is a description of the 600 block of the River City Mall. And, about all that is needed to make it an urban success is full-time residents—and hence, places for them to live, so, in late summer 1977 the city asked the Louisville-Jefferson County Downtown Development Corporation to fund a study to determine the feasibility of converting the upper stories of the buildings in this block into apartments. (In June 1978, the state announced plans for a $30,000 study of the 600 block.)

Students of cities already know that dwelling space is an essential element of any plan to save downtown—economically, one full-time resident is the equal of ten commuters. This is also one of the first humanly-scaled, sensibly-priced, and most-likely-to-succeed proposals suggested for downtown in a long time. For once, we are considering using existing resources, instead of sweeping away our history with giant development schemes.

Ironically, people won't venture downtown until it is both safe and commercially sound, and it cannot be that way until it has people. But, attractive apartments for professionals, students, and others along the River City Mall and other downtown streets might be just the catalyst that is needed.

Full-time residents would give the area stability and provide a sense of community, while the improved social environment created by them would also contribute to a better commercial climate by attracting better stores, restaurants, and movies. The improved shopping, along with higher class entertainment, would also be more inviting to tourists than the present dead after five-o'clock business district. In turn, the tourists would help businesses along the Mall, which would encourage more suburbanites to shop downtown. And so on.

And one attraction that might entice tourists from the cocoon of atrium-style hotels, glass-encased skyways, and windowless convention halls, is the rich architecture of the 600 block.

Lining both sides of the Mall, from the handsome Brown Hotel and the Commonwealth building on Broadway to the excruciatingly boring Lincoln Federal building at Chestnut street, is a range of richly decorated and often whimsical structures. A look above the storefront level of most of these buildings reveals all manner of elaborate details: masks, swags, finials, heraldic crests, colored tiles.

The five-story Berkeley Hotel, with its wide brick arches, carries on the local popularity of the Romanesque style, while the Kentucky Theatre employs Georgian motifs offset by glazed yellow brick. The Spanish Baroque Penthouse-United Artists theatre building is the crown of this downtown block and one of the great American movie-houses. The pink granite and bronze entrance of the Theatre Building, and the black glass and faceted facade of the Kentucky Pen Shop, are both enchanting and notable examples of the 1930s style known as Art Deco.

As a place to live, it is hard to believe that any suburban apartment complex could compete with such a combination of visual richness and a downtown location. But the new study intends to use the 600 block as a model or a prototype for other equally attractive and underutilized blocks, especially on Main Street.

After we have played with parking garages, malls, hotels, convention centers, and unilateral gargantuan panaceas, it is a sad commentary that we are only just beginning to study ways to enable Louisvillians to save downtown by living there. Yet, the apartment studies for the 600 block of the River City Mall—incredibly the only part of the central business district where no demolition or major new development is planned—may provide the answer to the question of how we can keep downtown Louisville alive.

Renovation May Be
Just Up Your Alley

OLD LOUISVILLE, the city's first historic district, was accorded national recognition in 1974 when it was named to the National Register of Historic Places, putting it in the same category as better known historic areas such as Beacon Hill in Boston and Georgetown in Washington, D.C. This designation was a tribute to the private individuals who, ten or fifteen years ago, began buying houses and restoring them. The on-going renovation of the Victorian houses in St. James and Belgravia Courts, and along Third and Fourth Streets, has brought young people and professionals back downtown at a time when most growth is to the suburbs, and has made the neighborhood one of the most desireable places in the city in which to live. Yet, as attractive and as pleasant as the blocks around Central Park have become, the neighborhood facelift has, until now at least, avoided whole sections of the area, namely the smaller streets and alleys that run behind almost all of the major throughfares in Old Louisville.

A good street map—or better yet, a tax map—of Old Louisville shows a network of alleys paralleling the main streets, a whole subculture of byways which, if developed imaginatively, could increase housing space and add considerably to the desirability of the neighborhood. At the moment, these alleyways are used primarily for parking, the garages fulfilling the same function as the carriage houses of earlier times. While some do indeed have apartments above them, many of these garages and outbuildings are in a state of disrepair. But, fixed up and renovated—or supplemented with sympathetic new building, these garage apartments could offer ideal urban dwellings. Just as the reconverted private stables of town houses—or "mews" as they are popularly called—have become among the most sought-after and most fashionable addresses in London, the same thing could happen here in Louisville.

The alleys of Old Louisville are rather neglected and down-at-the-heel looking, but there are a number of advantages to be gained by developing the mews concept. These secondary passages are far quieter and safer than the streets they parallel—it is possible to walk or ride a bicycle the length of Old Louisville, from Oak Street to the University, virtually unharassed by automobiles. And as traffic noise and pollution increase along the major commuting streets from Brook to Sixth, the alleys offer a privacy and a tranquility rarely associated with contemporary American urban living. One has only to experience the special quality of Belgravia Court—a street without automobiles or even a roadway—to realize how delightful such a prospect can be. There are other "streets," such as Floral Terrace, a tree-lined oasis hidden between Park Avenue and Ormsby, Sixth and Seventh Streets, that, with a little landscaping and paint could be transformed into another Belgravia.

To the urban planner (especially one concerned with the quality of cities that seems to have been lost in the age of the freeway) the chief attraction of the alleys of Old Louisville is that of scale; the bricks under foot, the narrowness reminiscent of medieval European cities, the two-story height of the garages, and often large shade trees, all contribute to a townscape that can be defined in human terms. Just as cars, trucks, and busses have claimed the asphalt of the neighborhood's main streets and have become the service arteries that the back streets once were, the alleys should become people spaces. Increasing the residential density of the area and having more people in the streets could also mean a safer neighborhood.

Even though one must think away the refuse and the deteriorating state of some of the buildings, it is possible to imagine handsome mews apartments linked to the main houses by gardens. The total effect would not be dissimilar to the charming narrow streets of London, Annapolis, or Charleston, South Carolina. Both imagination and money would be prerequisites of such development, but these passageways are yet another resource of Louisville's urban environment that should be tapped.

POSTSCRIPT. *In 1977, the National Endowment for the Arts awarded a grant to the city for a study of Louisville's alleys. Working with the Louisville Community Design Center, Grady Clay produced a book entitled* Alleys: A Hidden Resource *based on the Design Center's evaluation of five local alleys, including two in Old Louisville. The Design Center's proposals for one project, that in the Russell neighborhood of West Louisville, are being implemented.*

A brick paved alley in Old Louisville, this view taken between Third and Fourth Streets, Magnolia and Ormsby Streets

Widening the Expressway?

AWAITING the plan for the widening of the Watterson Expressway (the so-called "scaled-down" plan, the one that will displace only about 300 homes and businesses") is like contemplating a nightmare journey in a backward-spinning time machine.

It's hard to believe that Louisville is uniquely benighted with a clearly outmoded faith in highways as the answer to solving traffic problems. But then Louisville does have a penchant for being about twenty years behind other cities.

Almost as if there had been no energy crisis or no future threat of one, almost as if automobiles would continue to receive consideration over people, almost as if city centers weren't struggling from the disastrous effects of such planning fiascos as the Watterson, almost as if we still had an Eisenhower-like vision of the need for national defense evacuation routes, almost as if we were still living in the early 1960s, it is proposed that this metropolitan region have more asphalt added to the already too heavy choker of concrete that encircles it.

Some things, no matter how simple, seem to have to be stated again and again: Highways are generators of traffic, not alleviators of it; traffic, like water, seeks its own level. If we understand this basic principle, we don't need an expensive, slick planning study to tell us that a ten-lane Watterson is going to mean an increase in traffic of geometric proportions.

It also doesn't take expensive charts and a lot of planners' jargon to see how the interstate belt around Louisville is a chief reason for the decline of downtown. This giant asphalt serpent has spawned mini-cities and satellite clusters to the point where the Watterson has replaced the Ohio River as the main focus and primary artery of Louisville. Widening it will only aggravate the situation.

Incredibly, the highway people propose this kind of disruptive and totalitarian planning (by directing traffic flow you are defining growth in a very real way) and frankly announce that it could cost upwards of one hundred fifty million dollars—not to mention the additional cost of the Jefferson Freeway. At such a price, every taxpayer in the metropolitan area might do well to question what his money will be buying: a lot of asphalt, increased traffic, a more rapid deterioration of a downtown that is forced to compete against the powerful economics of the automobile, real estate, trucking and highway-building industries. What will result is a landscape more appropriate to Los Angeles than Kentucky.

And we haven't even begun to consider the increased air pollution. Still, some sort of award for gall ought to be presented to Kenneth E. Noll, the Tennessee consultant who concluded by a logic about as sound as those who claimed the earth was flat, that the wider the expressway is made, the more air pollution will be reduced.

[66]

The Watterson Expressway
looking west from Newburg Road

Superhighways are a superhoax. Yet Louisville is presented with a plan that is so monstrous in every way that no intelligent citizen or government official should even entertain the thought of its construction.

This is not to deny that there are legitimate planning problems regarding the automobile and the future shape of the city's growth. However, one hundred fifty million dollars would go a long way toward improving our transit system—the federal Urban Mass Transporation Administration has set aside only one hundred million dollars for experimental "urban automated people-mover systems"—or creating a new one based on rapid transit lines reaching the suburbs along spines running out from the city, not around it.

Unfortunately, Louisville's planning remains a planning for greedy machines (both automotive and political), not for people. But instead of lying down and playing dead before the automobile, we should accept the challenges of our growing community and come up with some unique, serious and long-lasting solutions to our planning problems.

Highway Planners Forgetting People

HIGHWAYS are probably the greatest single determinant in metropolitan Louisville's planned future.

The fate of all the well-intentioned proposals for cultural and other facilities downtown and the schemes for the redevelopment of the center city rest not on their own merits but with the people who plan, fund and build highways.

The interstates that bisect the city like the Berlin Wall and ring it like a noose have already changed the face of Louisville. By creating the major patterns of growth, the highways are a chief threat to the survival of downtown—and thus affect the future of the region as a whole. Yet the building of highways is almost as sacred to Americans as motherhood and apple pie. As in the case of defense spending, it seems somehow unpatriotic to question the wisdom of highway construction.

Except for occasional newspaper mention, the vitally important subject of highway planning is rarely discussed publicly, much less challenged in an objective and rational manner. If, as some argue, uncontrolled highway building contributes to the decline of both our cities and the quality of life, then we court disaster by our continued failure to address the problem.

It is especially puzzling that at a time when our city is struggling with dangerously polluted air and the nation is facing a critical—and perhaps permanent—shortage of fuel, public officials are seriously planning to spend millions of dollars not only to add more lanes to the Watterson Expressway, but to add even more miles of new highway, namely the Jefferson Freeway and the Southwest Radial.

How many times does it have to be stated that new highways do not decrease traffic, they only increase it?

If the Watterson Expressway is already congested, why should we spend one hundred sixty million dollars to make it many times more so? Why should we spend an additional two hundred million dollars to build a brand new Southwest Radial route which would only bring more cars, more congestion and more pollution to downtown Louisville? And are we really sure that we understand all the ramifications that a completed Jefferson Freeway (another loop of concrete to strangle the city) would have on the growth of the region?

Plans for the Southwest Radial, for example, are almost twenty years old. Unfortunately, the thinking behind such unbridled highway construction would seem to be at least that far out of date. This only points up the sad fact that the people who plan our future are hopelessly mired in an automobile-based philosophy which holds our city hostage.

Instead of putting so much money and misplaced faith in ribbons of asphalt, everyone involved with planning in Louisville and this state ought to be applying himself to alternatives to the automobile. Our emphasis should clearly be on efficient and pollution-free mass transportation.

In short, Louisville needs more imagination, not more cars and poisonous vapors.

"It is clear," says Phillip Johnson, one of America's most respected architects, "that our cities decay for the same reason that our air becomes polluted. We do not care enough." Even if this seems too harsh an indictment, it stresses the relationship between urban blight and automania.

If "care" is defined as the manifestation of our true feelings about our city, it is time to begin caring by taking a long, hard and realistic look at highway projects and by assessing their true cost.

POSTSCRIPT. *The Southwest Radial project has been temporarily shelved, partly because of strong citizen opposition.*

Shopping-Area "Towns": Sub-Urban Environment

DU PONT SQUARE is just one of the many "towns" spawned by suburban growth along Watterson Expressway and major arteries leading away from downtown Louisville. These clusters of shopping centers have assumed an importance almost greater than the city center around which they bloom, and they constitute the competition against which downtown is struggling. Collectively, they add up to a scattered, 1970s version of downtown.

Historically, cities have been located at natural breaks in transportation—the crossing of two trails, the meeting of two rivers, or a barrier to navigation, such as the Falls of the Ohio. Du Pont Square is located at the contemporary equivalent of such a break: The clover-leaf junction of Watterson Expressway and heavily traveled, four-lane Breckinridge Lane. Due to the automobile, such "new cities" are different from their predecessors in that the people they serve do not necessarily come from the immediate neighborhood. In fact, the shopping-center city competes not only with downtown, but with all the other centers similar to it in the metropolitan area.

This competition is fierce (nearby St. Matthews has evolved from a city in its own right to a thoroughfare for people on their way to other shopping areas), and in order to capture its share of the market, a shopping-center complex has to offer an ever-increasing range of services. In Du Pont Square one can find department stores, discount houses, banks, restaurants, bars, fast-food chains, health facilities (doctors, hospitals, even a spa), filling stations, car dealers, a building-supplies firm, offices, loan companies, sports facilities, entertainment (eight movie theaters), apartments and condominiums—most of the basic services with which one might define a city (funeral homes, schools and churches are still lacking). And, considering the number of people who depend on these services, it would be hard not to call Du Pont Square a city.

Yet, if Du Pont Square is a city in form, it is really not one in spirit. The image that the developers and merchants would like to project is that of a country town. With the exception of the hospitals and some of the office blocks, most of the buildings are only two stories high. A variety of styles—Cutesy Colonial, Highway Hacienda, Townehouse Tudor, Railroad Rococo—are employed in an attempt to create the environment of a small-town Main Street with an old-time flavor.

Newly built 'old' buildings, like Victoria Station, Ehrler's Dairy, Steak & Ale, Ollie's Trolley, or Sherwood Apartments, do provide a rather fun, if hardly notable, lineup of Pop architecture, but the necessity of providing parking around them isolates the buildings and weakens their impact. Even the First National Bank, the handsomest building in Du Pont Square, is like a piece of constructivist sculpture stranded on an asphalt wasteland.

Dutchman's Lane, the main thoroughfare of Du Pont Square

In short, Du Pont Square and the other shopping-center cities fall short of their goal of nostalgic ambience because their basic module is not a person on foot, but the automobile. While the idea of grouping several buildings in one complex offers more variety than the mall-under-one-roof concept, the chief disadvantage is that everything is too spread out, with a resulting loss of human scale. Du Pont Square is not for pedestrians; sidewalks are few and walking is difficult at best.

Many planners argue that the proliferation of such small satellite cities represents the city of the future, an auto-centered megalopolitan spread rather than a concentrated downtown. Du Pont Square may have taken many of the patrons from downtown Louisville, but such "cities" based on commerce alone cannot fabricate the history, the excitement, or the sense of identity of a two-hundred-year-old city.

Like the Lincoln Tower across Breckinridge Lane (the most urban form, the skyscraper, set in the most rural setting, the farm), Du Pont Square is a contradiction in terms that offers the benefits of neither crowded city nor pastoral countryside. Du Pont Square shows that it is possible to capture a superficial resemblance to a city, but it isn't the real thing.

[71]

Threatened Village Gives Sense of Community

VAN BUREN is a small Kentucky farming village nestled in the Salt River Valley at the mouth of Crooked Creek. Its dozen or so houses, general store, antique shop, church and cemetery are strung out along Kentucky Route 248 in Anderson County, just east of a point where Spencer and Nelson counties meet. Just beyond this main street is farmland, bottom land of the valley, framed by rolling hills.

Van Buren is not so very different from dozens of other farming communities in Kentucky—or throughout the South, for that matter. Its stark white clapboard church and its white frame houses are representative of a simple vernacular architecture. The church is the only building that doesn't need painting and the single-story brick building that once housed the Van Buren State Bank is used as a barn for farm horses. There is a mobile home and the ubiquitous junked car, but Van Buren is not unattractive. Most of all, it is a true rural village, a reminder of the idea of "community" too rarely attained in our cities and our suburbs.

Although named for an American president, no famous people were born here, nor are any state or national heroes buried in the small cemetery. And Van Buren is a town without a future, a village living under a sentence of extinction. Van Buren is scheduled to be covered by the waters of Taylorsville Lake, planned for construction by the U.S. Corps of Engineers.

This is not to suggest that a dam project which will back up twenty-two miles of river and which will flood several thousand acres is proceeding unchallenged. In fact, there is spirited local opposition and the Citizens Action Committee, based in Taylorsville, has filed suit against the Corps.

As in the campaign to save the Red River Gorge, history from before white settlement may help halt the damming of the Salt River Valley. In the immediate vicinity of Van Buren there are several potentially significant archaeological sites, some with associations perhaps as early as the archaic peoples of three thousand years ago. While archaeological sites have to be dug up, collated and interpreted, they do allow us some insight into the collective history of the past. But the village of Van Buren represents the thinnest, most fragile, and most vulnerable layer of time's record: our own.

In half a dozen years, if the Corps of Engineers prevails, Van Buren will remain only in photographs or in the memory of those who lived there or knew it first hand. The Taylorsville Lake will provide more than six thousand acres for boaters and sportsmen (mostly suburbanites from Jefferson County) and perhaps a small measure of flood control. But such projects should always be scrutinized, not only for the improvements they purportedly will offer, but for the true cost of those improvements.

Eleven miles west of Van Buren a sign announces that the Corps of

Rural Van Buren, Kentucky with its typical main street and grocery store is threatened with extinction

Engineers is "Building Tomorrow Today." Ironically, for that tomorrow, Kentucky will give up a lovely valley and its agricultural land and a rural village that links Kentuckians to their roots.

POSTSCRIPT. *Van Buren was completely abandoned shortly after this article appeared. However, in the spring of 1978 a federal judge halted construction on the Taylorsville Dam on the grounds that the Corps of Engineers' environmental impact statement did not adequately address such issues as psychological cost and the benefits of recreational area gained at the loss of farmland. After revising their impact statement, the Corps was granted permission to complete construction of the dam.*

III. PRESERVATION

Why Save the Whole Setting?

THE FATE of two Victorian houses formerly owned by the Woman's Club on South Fourth Street poses two fundamental questions: How do we decide what is worth preserving? And how do we reconcile our need for old buildings with the need for growth while still protecting individual rights and free economic initiative? More than the preservation of individual buildings, the issue really encompasses many of those elements which make a city a good or a bad place in which to live or visit.

Although outstanding examples of their style and period, the two brick houses are far more important as key elements in the fragile urban fabric. Their picturesque mass defines the boundaries between Central Park and the commercial part of Fourth Street, while their seemingly endless decorative details offer surprises and visual delight. To remove these houses from their neighborhood would be like pulling the keystone out of an arch.

That the case should go to the courts indicates that historic preservation in this country has finally come of age. Traditionally, preservation has meant the saving of individual monuments, the criteria usually having been sentimental associations with famous personages or events, artistic value, or belief that a building is representative of national culture. Obvious examples of this sort of preservation are Mount Vernon and Monticello, purchased and restored by private interests. Rarely have whole towns or districts been set aside in this manner. A notable exception is Williamsburg, although much of that was actually reconstruction rather than preservation, play-acting rather than history, artificial rather than real.

Today, fifty years after the restoration of Williamsburg was begun, preservation has moved to broader environmental and urban concerns. The battle to preserve the two houses demonstrates a new understanding that the man-made elements of the urban scene consist as much of spaces and the relationships between buildings as of the buildings themselves. Or, as Gordon Cullen wrote in his classic urban primer *The Concise Townscape* (1971), "one building is architecture, but two buildings are townscape."

No great city—Venice, Paris, Rome, London, Edinburgh—displays its architecture like pieces in a museum. In fact, what draws so many Americans to European towns and cities is not so much outstanding individual monuments, but innumerable groupings of second-rate buildings, arranged or developed in such a way as to produce an emotional response, an urban experience.

Romanesque Revival style house in the 1300 block of South Fourth Street, saved from demolition for a parking lot

In most European countries preservation is an instrument of national policy, backed up by government financing and strong legislation (unauthorized alteration of a landmark in France or Italy, for example,

can mean a stiff jail sentence). In rebuilding bombed-out cities, war-torn countries like Poland (which spends twenty-five percent of its housing budget on preservation and restoration) believe that the tangible evidence of the past is absolutely essential to the mental health of its populace. In Britain, where preservation is effected by private means, as it is here, the government supports conservation with tax laws, while the right to an historical past was recognized by the Civil Amenities Act of 1967.

American preservationists are beginning to adopt more sophisticated approaches modeled in part on European experience, with the result that places like Charleston, Annapolis, and Savannah, having demonstrated that commercial prosperity follows historic district zoning and adaptive use of older buildings, have become some of the most desirable cities in the country. But America, a country with the distinction of having destroyed its own cities, is still a novice in the field of preservation. Before this historian, or any other, can offer guidelines on *what* to save, we must alter some fundamental attitudes.

To begin with, we must understand that preservation and destruction are *not* equivalent alternatives, and that conservation is progressive, not reactionary. The vandals who destroy the past (in the name of "Progress") also destroy the future. Not only should they be prosecuted like polluters, but the destroyers—not the preservationists—should be the ones to prove conclusively that society will benefit from their actions.

Just as we have accepted the idea of the greater public good in, say, matters of national defense and health care, we must adopt the precept that the right to develop a piece of land belongs *not* just to the owner but to the public. The two brick Victorian houses at 1328 and 1332 South Fourth belong as much to the Old Louisville neighborhood and its residents as to the Woman's Club.

No preservationist really believes that everything must be preserved, but when notable examples of our physical heritage are destroyed they should be replaced with something better. If the two houses have outlived their usefulness then they should be replaced only by structures that maintain the streetscape, scale, and visual delight of the neighborhood.

Objectivity is difficult, often impossible, but we can begin by accepting the realization that no society, no association of human beings, as Kenneth Clark of *Civilisation* fame argues, "can cut itself off from its past or pull up its deepest roots without impoverishing or even destroying its spirit."

POSTSCRIPT. *The City of Louisville acquired the two houses by eminent domain (a national preservation first), an action that was unsuccessfully challenged by the Women's Club. The constitutionality of the Louisville Landmark Ordinance was upheld by the Kentucky Supreme Court—foreshadowing a similar ruling in June 1978 by the United States Supreme Court regarding Grand Central Terminal and the New York City landmarks law.*

Another of the brick Romanesque Revival houses on South Fourth Street rescued from the wrecker's ball

New Uses for the Old County Jail

JEFFERSON COUNTY JAIL, vacated when the handsome new Jefferson Hall of Justice was completed in 1976, was originally scheduled for demolition ("Progress thru Urban Renewal"), but fortunately it is now being considered for renovation for some other use.

Recognizing its landmark status (the jail was put on the National Register of Historic Places two years ago), County Judge Todd Hollenbach appointed a task force to study the feasibility of preserving and finding a suitable use for the old jail. It is to be hoped, even in the face of economic obstacles, that an imaginative solution to extend the life of this notable structure will be found. The jail must be preserved.

Although most citizens think of the jail in terms of its function rather than its architecture, the Jefferson County Jail is an integral part of the handsome and architecturally-significant government complex, formed by major buildings from several periods. The jail, along with the Jefferson County Courthouse, City Hall, and the new Hall of Justice, is a key element in the city's physical identity. The loss of the jail would do irreparable damage to the historical continuity of this unique grouping of civic buildings.

In terms of scale and streetscape, the loss of the jail would be a disaster. One can hardly imagine a modern steel and glass replacement of equal massiveness and picturesqueness. Downtown Louisville needs such strong buildings to define its streets and hold its corners; it certainly does not need another corner parking lot (like that already at Sixth and Liberty) or a new skyscraper isolated from the street by an anti-urban plaza.

Rarely is there strong support for the retention of a jail. Thus, some of the finest examples of American architecture have been torn down simply because they housed society's criminals. Yet jails are a fact of life, and we should perhaps recall that in the eighteenth and nineteenth centuries Americans led the world in both penal reform and prison design.

The Walnut Street Jail of 1773 in Philadelphia was the first penitentiary, based on the new humanitarian idea of individual confinement of prisoners. Half a century later, John Haviland built the Eastern State Penitentiary (also in Philadelphia) in which he exploited the radial plan, whereby cell blocks were arranged as spokes in a wheel. This arrangement, allowing for maximum security with a minimum of guard personnel, was so successful it was copied everywhere, giving Haviland the title of "Jailer to the World."

The Eastern State Penitentiary was designed in a Castellated Gothic style, the references to a medieval fortress were thought appropriate to incarceration. Haviland's later and more famous prisons, Moyamensing in Philadelphia and the Tombs in New York, were built in the Egyptian Revival style. Even more bleak and forbidding than those in the Gothic mode, the massive walls of such prisons were to remind the public of the hopelessness and eternity of penal entombment.

Although most of Haviland's best works have been destroyed, D. X. Murphy's Jefferson County Jail makes reference to both the Castellated and the Egyptian styles in the administrative wing and the cell-block, respectively. Such association may be out of favor in the twentieth century but it was seriously accepted in the nineteenth and is therefore important historically.

However, in deciding what future use to put the Jefferson County Jail, its present function should be disassociated from its considerable architectural and urbanistic merits. We are actually talking about just a name change, for this seventy-year-old building appears to be structurally

Old Jefferson County Jail. The castellated administration wing is to the left, the Egyptian-style cell-block to the right. A notable structure deserving suitable preservation

sound. There is no reason to assume that its service to the city and county should be terminated just because the jail facilities are being moved.

While further detailed study is needed to determine how best to use the jail, its design makes it obvious that it should be used for something that does not require a great deal of natural light—such as archival or record storage, or perhaps a museum.

Whatever use the building is put to, whether as a public facility, as an office or retail complex, or a combination of both, the important point is that the Jefferson County Jail, like the Big Four Bridge or the remaining commercial buildings on Main Street, is one of the resources of our urban environment whose future should be of vital interest to all Louisvillians.

POSTSCRIPT. *The County is now committed to preservation of the Old Jail. Washington developer Arthur Cotton Moore has been hired to prepare plans for possible adaptive re-use of the building.*

Phoenix Hill:
Next Preservation Target?

HISTORIC preservation appears to have come of age in Louisville. The city's commitment to preserving the past as the key to future development received national attention in a recent television presentation on preservation, where Louisville was chosen as the national prototype. *Louisville Magazine,* the Chamber of Commerce publication, has devoted an entire issue to local preservation.

Despite a temporary legal setback, the city has an active landmarks commission that is identifying and documenting individual buildings as well as whole districts whose preservation it deems essential to the well-being of the city. Mayor Harvey I. Sloane made preservation, particularly neighborhood rehabilitation, a major point in his administration. Restoration has meant renaissance for such areas as Old Louisville, Butchertown and the Cherokee Triangle.

Yet, in all this flurry of publicity, one of the most historic and interesting neighborhoods—Phoenix Hill—has been all but overlooked. Sometimes known as Clarksdale, Phoenix Hill is a fifty-block area of downtown bounded by Broadway, Baxter Avenue, Main and Hancock streets. In the past year, a community group, the Phoenix Hill Association, has led a clean-up campaign, but the area deserves far more attention—and assistance.

Phoenix Hill (which takes its name from a brewery and pleasure ground that served the German population of the district from 1865 to 1938) was developed almost simultaneously with downtown. It is older than Old Louisville or Butchertown and, in fact, contains some of the oldest remaining buildings in the city. Streets like Clay, Chestnut, Shelby, Liberty and Campbell are lined with many domestic structures from before the Civil War, some as early as the 1830s. These houses and several handsome churches whose spires give the district its own special skyline contribute to some of the best nineteenth century townscape in Louisville.

Today, Phoenix Hill's character is defined by pawn shops and automotive and industrial suppliers. Yet the commercial-residential mix gives the district a vitality not found in the streetcar suburbs of Old Louisville and the Highlands. But the truth is that Phoenix Hill is not a nice neighborhood. It is shabby and rundown—so much so that one wonders whether the city has perhaps written off the area.

Still, the community's supporters are the businesses located there. Restauranteur Don Grisanti has been a leading force behind the neighborhood association and the firms that call Phoenix Hill home—Casa Grisanti, Blatz and De Hart paint companies, Gatchel's photo supply store, and Bittner's Antiques & Interiors, for example, have considerable financial investment there.

Old houses help give this stretch of East Chestnut Street a special flavor, characteristic of the historic Phoenix Hill area

Admittedly, it requires more than the usual amount of imagination to picture what Phoenix Hill could look like, what it could become. But the nearby Butchertown block of Washington Street (between Shelby and Campbell) demonstrates the transformation that can be achieved by a little restoration and a lot of paint. The Home of the Innocents on Chestnut Street is an excellent example of how a new building can enhance the neighborhood and preserve the scale of the street.

Besides its architecture, Phoenix Hill's major asset is its close-to-downtown location. Its proximity to the eastward expanding Medical Center could make it an ideal quarter for doctors. In fact, with the economic commitment that such neightorhoods as Butchertown and Old Louisville have received, Phoenix Hill could almost become the Louisville equivalent of New Orleans's Vieux Carre.

Phoenix Hill is a Louisville resource that can be rescued, preserved and developed. But accomplishing this may be the toughest preservation challenge faced by Louisville so far.

POSTSCRIPT. *Even though Phoenix Hill's many handsome houses have yet to attract resident restoration, the now renovated old Ursuline Convent on Chestnut Street is acting as a catalyst for the area. The complex, known as the Cloister, features a number of restaurants, galleries, and boutiques and is proving a successful and popular attraction.*

[84]

Concrete vs. Cultural Heritage

THANKS to Louisville's lust for concrete and its business leaders' belief that parking lots are more important than a special urban ambiance, this city is about to lose another small but significant piece of its architectural and cultural heritage.

The Converse Building (more commonly known as the home of *The Christian Observer*) at 412 South Third Street is about to be demolished. In its place will be a parking lot that will accommodate twenty-five or thirty cars.

Before yet another piece of our city's heart is ripped out, and before the damage to our townscape caused by another open lot is inflicted, we ought to take a look at the Converse Building and at least assess our loss.

No single building makes a city, but the destruction of every individual structure takes a disproportionate chunk of our fragile urban fabric, with the result that our city is that much less identifiable, attractive and livable.

The one-hundred-year-old Converse Building was probably built originally as a house with the commercial first-floor facade added at a later date. Its handsome brick upper stories are topped by an elaborate cornice whose paired brackets mirror those on the old Customs House (now the Chamber of Commerce) next door.

The added cast-iron facade is an example of the American architectural genius that made it possible for nineteenth-century commercial buildings across the country to have the decorative stylistic features of New York and Europe. And, not coincidentally, cast iron represents a technological achievement that added significantly to the development of the skyscraper—America's greatest single contribution to world architecture.

In the middle of the last century cast-iron buildings similar to the Converse Building and those along West Main Street lined the commercial districts of most American cities. "Progress" spelled doom for most of these handsome structures and whole districts in cities like St. Louis and Cincinnati were eradicated.

Only because Louisville was a languishing southern city are we fortunate enough to have now the second largest collection of cast-iron architecture in the country. However, Louisville is catching up and is now intent on destroying the one architectural resource that gives this city distinction and makes it of interest to historians and travelers from America and abroad.

The Converse Building also has important historical associations in addition to architectural ones: Until recently it was the headquarters of *The Christian Observer,* the oldest religious newspaper in the country and perhaps one of the oldest in the world.

Architecture and history take a back seat to economics, and, as so often happens in Louisville, dollar return takes precedence over all other

considerations; imagination and the possibility of reasonable alternatives are casualties of a planning that puts dollars and cars ahead of people.

So, by a curious kind of logic, we are destroying part of downtown to bring people downtown; and when there is adequate parking downtown there will be nothing to drive downtown for.

Unfortunately, Louisville never asks the right questions, or else asks them only when it is too late. The real question here is whether Louisville and its people would be better served by a small cast-iron building rich in history or by more asphalt in a city that has far too little of the former and far too much of the latter.

POSTSCRIPT. *The Converse building was destroyed. While the owner did give the cast-iron pieces to the pieces to the Preservation Alliance, it is hard to believe that the retention of the building's facade would have interfered with the parking behind it.*

The century-old Converse Building on South Third Street, razed for a parking lot

The now-dismantled board-batten
Belknap Playhouse was originally
the chapel of the old House of
Refuge, as well as the centerpiece
of a notable picturesque landscape
composition. Photograph by Carl
Maupin

The Real Issue is Campus Planning

THE BELKNAP PLAYHOUSE at the University of Louisville has been in the news a lot lately. The school's master plan calls for its removal to make way for a new library. Moving the playhouse is opposed by preservationists, and they, the university, and the state have been working on an acceptable compromise. At this time, the fate of the playhouse is uncertain.

Many people may be surprised that a small board-and-batten theater and former reform-school chapel is the subject of such controversy. But the stakes are far higher than the structure's future.

The real issue is not the playhouse, but a campus planning policy that might allow the destruction of the oldest and prettiest part of the university. This raises questions about the master plan and how the university regards its role as a guardian of a cultural legacy.

"What should we preserve?" is a question that this city has been forced to ask with increasing frequency and urgency. There is no simple answer, but in a recent book, *The Future of the Past,* British architectural critic Osbert Lancaster offers three grounds on which we are logically entitled to press for preservation, and these are applicable to the playhouse.

The first, aesthetic merit of the individual building, is the most difficult to assess, and there is certainly argument over the intrinsic merit of the playhouse. Time, perhaps, is the only true judge of taste, for what is beautiful to one generation is often ugly to the next. Yet the playhouse is representative of the rural Gothic style once so popular in this country.

The second criterion for preservation is emotional attachment. Proof of strong emotional ties to the playhouse is provided by the interest over the building's fate and the affection with which it is regarded in the community. Most people revere it as a theater, but it is also a symbol of the campus and a reminder of the university's predecessor here, the House of Refuge.

Third, and most important, a building is worthy of preservation if it fulfills a vital role in the landscape—in its setting or ambiance. Here again, the playhouse has an exceptionally strong case.

In fact, it is the entire setting that is the real issue, for the playhouse is an integral part of the oldest section of campus, probably the work of the Olmsted Brothers, the internationally famous landscape architects. Its collection of several species of handsome trees makes it virtually an arboretum. Most of all, this park-like landscape facing Third Street is the most abiding image of the university for the community. As such, the playhouse and its surroundings should be inviolate.

In a spirit of compromise and cooperation, a number of proposals have been put forth to solve the dilemma of the playhouse and reconcile it with the need for a new library.

It has been suggested that the playhouse be moved to another site on campus or even off campus. Less drastic, but potentially more destructive, are proposals to move the playhouse slightly westward to accommodate the library or to incorporate the playhouse into the new library design.

The latter proposal is an ingenious solution, but it ignores the larger issue. And, while a short move might seem less harmful, the playhouse should not be moved at all.

Given the importance of the total setting, the arguments should focus on the library, not the playhouse. It is just simply the wrong place to locate the new library. No matter how modest at first, libraries tend to grow, and such a building where intended would mean the eventual destruction of the site.

It is really unnecessary that the fate of the playhouse be tied up with the placement of the library. The current controversy points up the inflexibility of the new campus plan and the limited vision of planners who want to complete a quadrangel merely because symmetry looks good on paper.

This is especially lamentable when one considers that the library could be better located to begin with. One obvious place is behind the present library, on the site now occupied by the Fine Arts building and other temporary war-time structures and the Women's Gymnasium.

Situated there, the new building could be connected to the old library and still be at the center of campus.

A growing university has to build new buildings and sometimes tear down old ones but how many schools would destroy their most-beloved building and eradicate their loveliest open space?

Universities are training grounds for the future, but they also bear a responsibility as repositories of the past. Or, as William Morris said around the time the Belknap Playhouse was built: "Old buildings do not belong to us . . . They are not in any sense our property, to do as we like with. We are only trustees for those who come after us."

POSTSCRIPT. *Although Belknap campus is a National Register Historic District, The University took down the playhouse in 1977, claiming that they intend to re-erect it at another location at a future date.*

Preserving a Visual Memory Bank

THE FUTURE of the past along downtown Louisville's West Main Street would seem to be assured. The restoration of such buildings as the Natural History Museum and the Hart Block has brought national recognition. So it might be assumed that the district's rich commercial heritage would be a keystone in future development along the city's riverfront.

However, nomination of the 100 block of West Main Street to the National Register of Historic Places has raised some questions in the minds of property owners along the block's south side. Concern has been expressed about the historical value of these buildings and the reasons for their inclusion in an historic district. Owners wonder about the responsibilities that such a designation might entail, and whether National Register status might restrict them from freely developing their properties.

Admittedly, the south side of the 100 block does not present a streetscape of contiguous facades as does the obviously valuable north side. But its inclusion in an historic district is nonetheless justified on the grounds that the remaining buildings collectively contribute to Louisville's historical identity. The old buildings along West Main Street from First to Ninth Streets constitute a visual memory bank, they are a physical history lesson, and they are living reminders of Louisville's past and of its commercial growth.

As is the case with so many historic districts in Louisville and elsewhere, the whole is greater than the sum of its individual parts. While very few of these handsome masonry and cast iron buildings can of themselves claim outstanding architectural importance or identification with a single major historical event, the district concept is intended to assist in our recognition of the greater fabric of our urbanscape. Seen in this context, it would be a mistake to exclude the south side of the 100 block from the Main street historic district.

One of the chief reasons that Louisville's waterfront area has retained so much of its past is due to its commercial eclipse in the early twentieth century. Had we experienced the tremendous growth of cities such as New York or Atlanta, we might have lost much of what today makes Louisville so special. Still, Main Street, is only a ghost of what it was a few decades ago.

One might argue that new buildings, such as the Farm Credit Bank, the Galt House, and the First National Tower, were economically necessary. But only rarely has such new construction been the result of intelligent discussion weighing the loss of the past against the benefits of its replacement.

So much of the planning of cities—whether preservation or highway construction—is a matter of choice. However, the reasons for the choices

have too often been only the financial gain of the developers, rather than consideration of the greater public good.

Perhaps part of the concern of property owners is based on a lack of knowledge of preservation law, in this case the National Register of Historic Places. National Register listing carries little or no restrictions. Although the Advisory Council on Historic Preservation is entitled to comment on the effect of any federally financed projects, the property owner is basically free to do whatever he wishes with his property. However, matching federal grants are available for restoration.

In fact, the only real onus on the property owner is that of public opinion. As American laws do not allow jail terms for landmark destruction (as they do in other civilized countries), the National Register's primary goal is the identification of those buildings, sites, and objects which are deemed worthy of preservation as important reminders of the history of a city, state, or nation.

To point out those structures and places which speak to our spiritual and psychological needs and suggest that they be retained is seen by some as a frontal attack on basic American freedoms. Yet the limited restrictions of National Register designation are far less restrictive than building and fire codes, zoning laws, or the 55 mph speed limit.

Nobody wants any more governmental regulation, yet we accept necessary expenses and inconvenience in areas like public health and military defense as vital to the common good.

Designation of the few remaining buildings along the south side of the 100 block of West Main Street (and adjoining structures on First Street) is consistent with the wishes of a society to preserve the best of its past.

Handsome Victorian facades of two commercial buildings in the 100 block of West Main Street help contribute to a sense of historical identity

We Need Our Physical Past

THERE IS a battle raging for the heart of downtown Louisville. Everyone agrees that the central business district is not as healthy as it should be, but there is a wide variety of views on how it should be resuscitated—ranging from the preservationist's brand of faith healing to the Center City Commission's heart transplant medicine.

Symptomatic of the lack of unified planning philosophy is the current controversy over the building to be erected at Sixth and Main Streets (with its "pedway") and the possible development of a multimillion-dollar "galleria" in the Walnut-Liberty-Fourth street area which will stir proponents and opponents.

A basic problem regarding the planning process in Louisville is that planning decisions are made by a visually unlearned plutocracy whose inclination is to think that bonds, tall buildings, and parking lots make a city. Couple this with Louisville's lack of nerve and imagination ("If you're good, you must be from someplace else"), and the result is planning in which the public is served last.

It is, however, possible to have our urbanistic cake and eat it too; it is possible to save downtown and to encourage new development. There is no reason for name-calling and bitterness, and there are very good reasons why preservationists and bankers should work together. A successful downtown area needs the density that would be provided both by saving existing structures and by adding new ones. Urban conservation is good business; it has proven the best resource for redevelopment in other cities and can do so here.

We need our physical past to remind us who we are, just as we need that unique sense of place that is Louisville. But unfortunately we have tended to think of preservation or development in absolute terms, and with such polarization has come a lack of confidence in the special character of the city.

While it is obviously impossible to save everything, sweeping proposals that feature eradication of entire blocks negate all that intelligent city planning should be—such advocates recall the American Army colonel in Vietnam who said: "We had to destroy the village in order to save it."

Our lack of self-confidence is an affliction that we might call "Atlantaisis." Its major symptom is a desire to save the city by remaking it into a plastic and asphalt copy of the sun-belt metropolis. In our quest to be "modern" and "up to date" (instead of just being Louisville), we have shied away from being adventurous and have grabbed for the mediocre and the second-rate of those cities we think we should emulate.

While never asking what is great about Louisville, we have proclaimed that "Conventions are Great in Lousville" and have asked people with party hats and noisemakers from Akron and Peoria to help save

City Hall. "We may be able to live and worship without architecture," as Victorian critic John Ruskin remarked, "but we cannot remember without architecture." Our physical past is essential to our self-identity, and hence our well-being

downtown by booking our "new" convention center. Through sacrifice of the Tyler Block (called one of the finest 19th-century commercial blocks in the entire country) on the altar of Atlanta worship, the convention center will be joined by a seventeen-story atrium-style hotel—a cliché old even in Atlanta.

Yet there is nothing "wrong" about a new hotel downtown—in fact, it is something to be welcomed. What is sad is that Louisville could have had *both* the Tyler Block and a new hotel.

And now the Will Sales building at Liberty and the River City Mall is threatened. Formerly the Courier-Journal building, this outstanding example of Second Empire Revival style is one of the most significant structures remaining in this city. Why is it threatened? Because it is old, and dirty, and Victorian, and because we lack the imagination to propose its reuse. It is an important link to our past, and it could be an ideal focal point for the Fourth Street mall or a galleria.

There is room enough downtown for new construction without destruction—stack the cars but not the people. Place a seventeen-story hotel or a 40-story office tower on its side (maybe behind existing facades) and you can revitalize several downtown blocks.

There is no neat definition of what makes a successful urban experience, but we can point to key elements of density and diversity, civic spirit and identity.

We can state that a slick, packaged vision of tomorrow is not as important as tolerating and encouraging variety and fostering human contact and human scale. And we can urge this city to demand the highest standard of architectural design—retaining the best older buildings while commissioning the best new ones. We can start by holding national or international architectural competitions for major buildings, instead of settling for the lowest common denominator as we do now.

Most of all, Louisville must accept the principle that the planning of a city is an equation into which economics is only one factor, and that when public good comes before private profit everyone will benefit.